Spring's Whispers

Matthew Petchinsky

Spring's Whispers

Spring's Whispers: The Groundhog's Prediction

By: Matthew Petchinsky

Introduction: How the Groundhog's Prediction Shapes Our Perception of Spring

Every year on February 2nd, countless people across North America turn their attention to a small, furry creature stepping cautiously out of its burrow. With a keen eye on whether it casts a shadow, we collectively wait for what this moment might signify: either six more weeks of winter or the promise of an early spring. Groundhog Day, a tradition rooted in folklore and celebration, has transcended its humble origins to become a cultural phenomenon, shaping how we anticipate the arrival of spring.

But how does this ritual, seemingly whimsical and unscientific, hold such sway over our imaginations? What is it about the groundhog's prediction that resonates so deeply with our hopes for renewal and warmth? To answer these questions, we must explore not only the event's folkloric roots but also its symbolic and psychological implications.

The Groundhog as a Seasonal Harbinger

The groundhog's unique role as a predictor of seasonal transitions is steeped in tradition. Emerging from hibernation in the depths of winter, it symbolizes the first glimmers of spring's approach. The simplicity of this act—whether the groundhog sees its shadow or not—offers a strikingly clear answer to a complex question: Is spring near?

In a world increasingly dominated by precise weather forecasts and scientific data, this tradition provides a comforting ritual that connects us to nature in an intuitive and almost magical way. By focusing on a single animal and its interaction with the elements, we collectively project our hopes and fears onto a natural occurrence, creating a sense of shared anticipation.

The Psychological Appeal of Groundhog Day

At its core, the groundhog's prediction taps into universal human emotions: hope and resilience. Winter, with its cold and often bleak landscapes, is a time of endurance. People eagerly await spring, not just as a change in weather but as a metaphorical rebirth. The groundhog, stepping into the spotlight on February 2nd, becomes an embodiment of that yearning.

Psychologically, rituals like Groundhog Day provide comfort and structure. The act of looking to the groundhog for guidance mirrors humanity's long-standing need to find patterns and meaning in the natural world. Whether or not the groundhog's prediction proves accurate, the tradition offers an optimistic lens through which we can view the transition between seasons.

Cultural Significance and Shared Experience

Groundhog Day is more than a quirky event—it is a cultural touchstone that fosters a sense of community. Whether in Punxsutawney, Pennsylvania, where the celebration draws thousands of visitors, or in living rooms across the continent, the day invites people to come together in celebration of a shared tradition.

The event also reflects the timeless human tendency to blend science, superstition, and storytelling. Though few seriously rely on the groundhog's prediction as a reliable weather forecast, its symbolism is powerful. The groundhog is not just an animal—it is a narrative device that shapes how we talk about and experience the shift from winter to spring.

Spring as a Symbol of Renewal

Spring's arrival has always been a time of great significance in human culture, representing new beginnings, growth, and the triumph of life over the harshness of winter. The groundhog's prediction, therefore, carries more weight than a simple weather forecast—it encapsulates the anticipation of transformation.

This symbolism resonates particularly in modern times, as people seek hope amid the stresses of daily life. The groundhog's emergence becomes a touchpoint for optimism, reminding us that no matter how cold or dark the winter, warmth and light are on the horizon.

Critiques and Modern Interpretations

In recent years, the accuracy of the groundhog's predictions has been called into question, with meteorological studies showing little correlation between the animal's shadow-based forecast and actual weather patterns. However, this lack of scientific precision has done little to diminish the event's popularity. In fact, the tradition endures precisely because it is not about accuracy—it is about belief and connection.

In a broader context, Groundhog Day also invites reflection on humanity's relationship with nature. As we face increasingly erratic weather patterns due to climate change, the idea of a single animal predicting the seasons feels both nostalgic and poignant. The groundhog's role as a symbol of seasonal shifts reminds us of the interconnectedness of all life and the delicate balance of ecosystems.

The Groundhog's Legacy in Shaping Perceptions

Groundhog Day's enduring appeal lies in its ability to bridge the gap between folklore and modernity, offering a playful yet profound way to mark the changing of the seasons. By shaping how we perceive the arrival of spring, it transforms the mundane passage of time into an event imbued with meaning and anticipation.

This introduction lays the groundwork for a deeper exploration of the groundhog's role in seasonal transitions. As we delve into the chapters ahead, we will uncover the intricate layers of this tradition—its historical origins, ecological significance, and enduring place in the cultural imagination. From the shadow it casts to the hope it inspires, the groundhog's prediction is much more than a weather forecast; it is a lens through which we view the inevitable cycles of nature and our place within them.

Chapter 1: The Role of the Groundhog in Seasonal Transitions

Throughout history, humanity has sought to understand and predict the changing of the seasons. Among the most peculiar and enduring traditions in this pursuit is the celebration of Groundhog Day, where a small burrowing animal becomes the focal point of weather lore and seasonal shifts. This chapter explores the cultural, ecological, and symbolic significance of the groundhog in marking and influencing seasonal transitions, delving into its origins, scientific basis, and enduring legacy.

The Groundhog: A Seasonal Symbol

The groundhog, also known as a woodchuck or marmot, is a member of the squirrel family (Sciuridae) and a native of North America. Its behaviors, particularly its hibernation patterns, have long been associated with the rhythms of nature. In winter, the groundhog retreats into its burrow, entering a state of torpor that conserves energy during the cold months. This biological adaptation made it a natural candidate for folkloric interpretation as a herald of spring.

The tradition of Groundhog Day, celebrated annually on February 2nd, elevates the groundhog to the role of a weather oracle. According to legend, if the groundhog emerges from its burrow and sees its shadow, it retreats, signaling six more weeks of winter. If it does not see its shadow, an early spring is foretold. While the science behind this tradition is minimal, its cultural resonance endures.

Historical and Cultural Roots

The origins of Groundhog Day trace back to ancient European traditions, particularly the Celtic festival of Imbolc, which celebrated the midway point between the winter solstice and spring equinox. This festival was associated with fertility, weather divination, and the goddess Brigid. In Germany, this evolved into Candlemas, where clergy blessed candles and rural communities observed hedgehogs or badgers as weather predictors.

German immigrants brought these customs to America, where the groundhog replaced the hedgehog due to its abundance and similar habits. The first official Groundhog Day was celebrated in Punxsutawney, Pennsylvania, in 1887, solidifying the groundhog's role as a cultural icon. Today, Punxsutawney Phil, the world's most famous groundhog, draws crowds and media attention, underscoring the tradition's blend of folklore and festivity.

The Groundhog's Ecological Importance

Beyond its folkloric role, the groundhog plays a significant ecological part in seasonal transitions. As a burrowing mammal, it contributes to soil aeration and nutrient cycling. Its activity influences plant growth and provides habitats for other species, such as rabbits and snakes. The groundhog's hibernation schedule is also an indicator of seasonal changes, as it responds to temperature and daylight shifts.

Scientific studies of groundhog behavior have provided valuable insights into hibernation, a phenomenon of interest in fields ranging from climate science to medicine. By understanding how groundhogs regulate body temperature and conserve energy, researchers hope to uncover applications for human health, such as treatments for hypothermia or advancements in long-term space travel.

Symbolism and the Human Connection

The groundhog symbolizes the interplay between humanity and nature, reflecting our desire to predict and adapt to the environment. Its emergence from the burrow mirrors humanity's yearning for renewal and the end of harsh winters. The Groundhog Day tradition encapsulates a blend of hope, humor, and connection to the natural world.

Furthermore, the groundhog's role in seasonal transitions resonates with themes of transformation and resilience. Just as the groundhog adapts to the demands of each season, so too must humans adjust their lives to the ever-changing rhythms of nature. The celebration of Groundhog Day invites reflection on these cycles and our place within them.

Modern Perspectives on Groundhog Day

While the tradition of Groundhog Day is steeped in folklore, modern perspectives often regard it as a lighthearted cultural event rather than a serious meteorological prediction. Nonetheless, its popularity has spurred interest in climate science and the impacts of seasonal transitions. Observing the groundhog serves as a reminder of the interconnectedness of all life and the subtle signs that nature provides.

In an era of environmental change, the groundhog's symbolic emergence highlights the need to respect and protect ecosystems. By preserving the habitats of species like the groundhog, humanity ensures the continuity of these natural indicators and the wisdom they offer about seasonal patterns.

Groundhogs are more than mere mascots for a quirky holiday; they embody the intricate relationship between nature, culture, and science. In the chapters that follow, we will delve deeper into the groundhog's biology, the origins of its lore, and the broader implications of seasonal transitions for human life and the environment. From ancient rituals to modern celebrations, the groundhog's role as a bridge between worlds remains as compelling as ever.

Chapter 2: The Whisper of Spring: Hope and Renewal

As winter loosens its grip and the first signs of spring emerge, a profound transformation begins to unfold in both nature and the human spirit. This chapter explores the deeper significance of spring as a season of hope and renewal, examining its impact on our emotions, traditions, and relationship with the natural world. Through the lens of folklore, science, and culture, we will uncover why spring resonates so deeply with humanity as a time of rebirth and possibilities.

The Symbolism of Spring: A Universal Archetype

Spring has long been regarded as a metaphor for renewal and hope. Across cultures and epochs, the season's arrival is celebrated as a victory over the stagnation and hardships of winter. This transition is not merely about warmer weather—it is a profound shift in energy and opportunity.

In mythology, spring is often depicted as a time when life triumphs over death. The Greek myth of Persephone, for instance, symbolizes the return of growth and fertility after the barren winter months. Her emergence from the underworld marks the reawakening of the Earth, a narrative echoed in countless other cultural traditions. Similarly, agricultural societies celebrated spring as the season when crops began to grow, securing their survival.

Spring's archetypal energy extends beyond folklore. It speaks to a universal human experience: the desire for change, growth, and transformation. As the days grow longer and the air warms, spring awakens not only the natural world but also a sense of optimism and renewal in the human heart.

Hope in the Face of Adversity

Spring's significance as a symbol of hope is particularly powerful because it follows the challenges of winter. The harsh cold, limited daylight, and scarcity of resources associated with winter can mirror personal struggles and periods of stagnation. Spring, then, becomes a beacon of possibility, a reminder that difficult times are temporary and brighter days lie ahead.

The psychological impact of this seasonal transition cannot be overstated. Studies have shown that longer daylight hours and warmer temperatures contribute to improved mood and increased energy levels. Known as the "spring awakening," this phenomenon reflects the deep connection between environmental changes and human well-being.

This seasonal shift offers a natural metaphor for resilience. Just as flowers push through frozen ground to bloom, individuals can overcome challenges and start anew. The whisper of spring, carried on the first mild breezes of the season, tells us that renewal is possible and hope is justified.

Renewal in Nature: A Celebration of Life

Spring is, above all, a celebration of life. The season brings an explosion of activity in the natural world, from the return of migratory birds to the budding of trees and the blooming of flowers. This resurgence of life is a reminder of the Earth's regenerative power.

In agricultural terms, spring is the time to sow seeds, both literally and metaphorically. Farmers prepare their fields, planting crops that will sustain them through the year. Gardeners cultivate their soil, anticipating the growth that will follow. This act of planting embodies faith in the future—a belief that the effort invested now will bear fruit later.

From an ecological perspective, spring marks a critical phase in many species' life cycles. Animals emerge from hibernation, birds build nests, and insects pollinate the first flowers of the season. These interconnected processes illustrate the delicate balance of ecosystems and highlight the importance of preserving the natural world.

Spring in Cultural and Spiritual Practices

The arrival of spring has inspired rituals and celebrations across the globe, reflecting its importance as a time of hope and renewal. Festivals like Ostara, Holi, and Easter honor the season's themes of rebirth, fertility, and transformation. These traditions often include symbols of new life, such as eggs, flowers, and young animals.

In Wiccan and pagan practices, the spring equinox—when day and night are of equal length—is a sacred time. Known as Ostara, this festival honors balance and fertility, celebrating the return of the sun and the fertility of the Earth. Rituals often include planting seeds, lighting candles, and offering thanks to deities associated with growth and abundance.

Spring also plays a significant role in personal and communal renewal. Spring cleaning, for instance, is more than a household chore—it is a symbolic act of clearing away the old to make room for the new. Similarly, many cultures mark the season with acts of charity, community building, and self-improvement.

The Emotional Landscape of Spring

Spring's ability to inspire hope and renewal extends to our emotional and psychological lives. The season's longer days and increased sunlight stimulate the production of serotonin, a hormone associated with happiness and well-being. This physiological response is mirrored in the cultural associations of spring with positivity and growth.

For many, spring is a time to set new goals and embrace change. Just as nature undergoes a transformation, individuals feel encouraged to shed old habits, start new projects, and pursue personal growth. The phrase "a spring in one's step" captures this sense of buoyancy and optimism.

Moreover, spring offers an opportunity to reconnect—with nature, with others, and with oneself. Outdoor activities, gardening, and communal events foster a sense of belonging and revitalization. These connections are crucial for mental and emotional health, reinforcing spring's role as a season of holistic renewal.

Challenges and Opportunities in Renewal

While spring is often associated with hope, its promise of renewal also requires effort and adaptability. Just as seeds must be nurtured to grow, personal and collective renewal demands commitment and action. The transition from winter to spring is not always smooth—unexpected frosts, storms, or delays in growth can serve as reminders that renewal is a process, not an instant transformation.

This tension between promise and effort underscores an important lesson: renewal is an ongoing journey. Spring invites us to embrace challenges as opportunities for growth, trusting in the cycle of life and the resilience of nature.

The Whisper of Spring: A Call to Action

Spring's arrival is more than a change in weather—it is a call to action. It invites us to reflect on what we wish to cultivate in our lives and to take the first steps toward achieving those goals. Whether through planting literal seeds in a garden or metaphorical seeds in the form of new ideas and endeavors, spring encourages us to invest in the future.

As the natural world comes alive with possibility, so too can we awaken to our own potential. The whisper of spring carries a message of hope and renewal, reminding us that no matter how harsh the winter, new beginnings are always possible.

In the chapters to come, we will continue to explore the themes of seasonal transitions and their profound impact on our lives. From the role of tradition to the science of seasonal changes, we will uncover the many ways in which the whisper of spring inspires growth and transformation.

Chapter 3: When Predictions Go Wrong: Adapting to Change

The arrival of spring, heralded by rituals like Groundhog Day and other seasonal traditions, often brings with it a sense of expectation and hope. However, as with any attempt to predict the future—whether it be through folklore, meteorology, or personal plans—there is always the possibility that predictions will go awry. This chapter examines how unexpected outcomes, whether in weather patterns, personal goals, or broader societal events, challenge us to adapt and thrive despite uncertainty. Through the lens of resilience and adaptability, we'll explore how embracing change can lead to growth and opportunity.

The Limitations of Prediction

Predicting the future, especially in relation to natural phenomena, is inherently uncertain. Despite advances in meteorology and climate science, the weather remains subject to a complex interplay of variables that defy absolute certainty. Similarly, traditions like Groundhog Day, while charming and symbolic, offer no guarantees about the onset of spring.

In the face of inaccurate predictions, frustration and disappointment are natural reactions. We invest emotionally in forecasts because they provide a sense of control over an uncertain future. When these expectations are unmet—such as when an early spring prediction is followed by weeks of harsh cold—it can feel as though nature itself has betrayed us.

Yet, this uncertainty is not without purpose. The unpredictability of life serves as a reminder of our limitations and the need to cultivate flexibility in our expectations. By recognizing the limits of prediction, we can shift our focus from controlling outcomes to preparing for a range of possibilities.

Lessons from Nature: Resilience in the Face of Uncertainty

Nature offers countless examples of resilience and adaptation to unpredictable circumstances. Plants and animals, for instance, have evolved strategies to cope with sudden changes in their environments. A late frost might damage some crops, but others, such as cold-hardy plants, will survive and even thrive.

Groundhogs themselves are emblematic of this adaptability. Their hibernation patterns, while influenced by environmental cues, include built-in flexibility to account for fluctuating conditions. If food is scarce or temperatures drop unexpectedly, they can extend their torpor, conserving energy until circumstances improve.

These natural strategies provide a powerful metaphor for human resilience. Just as ecosystems adapt to changes beyond their control, individuals and communities can learn to navigate uncertainty by cultivating flexibility, resourcefulness, and persistence.

When Plans Derail: Personal Resilience in Uncertain Times

Unmet expectations are not confined to weather forecasts—they extend to every aspect of life. Whether it's a delayed goal, an unexpected career setback, or a personal challenge, the experience of plans going awry is universal. The key to overcoming these moments lies in how we respond.

1. **Acknowledging Disappointment:** It's important to allow space for processing emotions when predictions fail or plans falter. Disappointment, frustration, and even grief are valid responses that pave the way for growth.

2. **Reframing the Situation:** Shifting perspective can transform setbacks into opportunities. For example, a prolonged winter may provide more time for indoor projects or self-reflection, while an unexpected challenge can inspire creative problem-solving.

3. **Building Flexibility:** Flexibility is the cornerstone of resilience. By remaining open to alternative paths and outcomes, we can reduce the impact of unexpected changes and find new ways to achieve our goals.

4. **Drawing on Support:** Community and connection are vital in times of uncertainty. Sharing experiences and seeking advice or encouragement can provide the strength needed to adapt and move forward.

Cultural Adaptations to Seasonal Variability

Throughout history, cultures worldwide have developed practices to cope with and adapt to the unpredictability of seasonal transitions. These adaptations often reflect a deep understanding of natural cycles and a willingness to embrace change.

For example:

- **Agricultural Practices:** Farmers historically planted diverse crops to hedge against unpredictable weather, ensuring that at least some would survive adverse conditions.
- **Seasonal Festivals:** Many traditions, such as the Celtic Imbolc or Japanese Cherry Blossom Festival, celebrate the changing seasons without rigid expectations, focusing instead on themes of renewal and gratitude.
- **Proverbs and Folklore:** Weather-related sayings, like "March comes in like a lion and goes out like a lamb," acknowledge variability and encourage patience through transitional periods.

By embedding adaptability into cultural practices, these traditions offer valuable lessons in resilience and acceptance.

Scientific Advances and the Role of Uncertainty

In modern times, advancements in meteorology and climate science have significantly improved our ability to predict weather and seasonal changes. Yet, even the most sophisticated models cannot eliminate uncertainty. Factors such as microclimates, unexpected storms, or long-term climate shifts remind us that nature is dynamic and often unpredictable.

Rather than seeking perfection in predictions, science encourages a probabilistic approach: planning for a range of scenarios rather than a single outcome. This mindset, when applied to everyday life, can reduce the shock of unexpected events and foster proactive, adaptable strategies.

Adapting to Broader Changes: Climate and Society

In an era of global climate change, the importance of adaptability has never been more apparent. Seasonal patterns are becoming less predictable, with late frosts, prolonged droughts, and unseasonable storms disrupting traditional cycles. These shifts challenge both natural ecosystems and human societies to adapt on unprecedented scales.

For individuals, this might mean reassessing habits and routines, such as energy use or food sourcing. For communities, it requires innovation and collaboration to build resilience against future uncertainties. Groundhog Day, while lighthearted, serves as a reminder of our connection to these broader changes and the need to respond with foresight and flexibility.

The Opportunity in Uncertainty

While unpredictability can be daunting, it also holds the potential for growth and discovery. When predictions go wrong, they challenge us to reevaluate our assumptions, learn from the experience, and emerge stronger. Adapting to change fosters creativity and resourcefulness, qualities that are essential for navigating a complex and ever-changing world.

For example:

- An unexpected snowfall might inspire innovative solutions for staying warm or finding new ways to enjoy the season.
- A delayed project deadline can provide the opportunity to refine and improve the final product.
- A personal setback might open doors to paths previously unconsidered.

These moments, while challenging, ultimately reinforce the value of adaptability as a skill for thriving in uncertain times.

Conclusion: Embracing the Unpredictable

When predictions go wrong, whether they involve a groundhog's shadow or life's greater uncertainties, they remind us of a fundamental truth: change is inevitable, and our ability to adapt is our greatest strength. By embracing flexibility, drawing on resilience, and finding opportunity in the unexpected, we can navigate even the most uncertain transitions with grace and confidence.

As we move forward, let us take inspiration from nature's resilience and humanity's capacity for innovation. The challenges posed by unpredictable events are not obstacles to be feared but opportunities to grow, adapt, and thrive. Just as the groundhog emerges each year to face the unknown, so too can we meet the future with courage and hope.

Chapter 4: The Groundhog as a Symbol of Hope

Few animals hold the cultural significance of the groundhog, particularly in its role as a weather predictor and herald of seasonal change. On Groundhog Day, February 2nd, this unassuming burrower emerges from its winter retreat to deliver its annual forecast, an act steeped in folklore and tradition. While the scientific accuracy of this ritual is negligible, the groundhog's role transcends its shadow. It has become a powerful symbol of hope, renewal, and the enduring optimism that accompanies the transition from winter to spring.

In this chapter, we explore how the groundhog has come to embody hope, examining its historical, cultural, and psychological significance. We also consider the broader implications of the groundhog's symbolism in a world increasingly marked by uncertainty and the need for resilience.

Historical Roots of the Groundhog as a Symbol

The groundhog's association with hope and renewal is deeply rooted in history. This connection begins with the ancient European traditions from which Groundhog Day evolved, such as the Celtic festival of Imbolc and the Christian observance of Candlemas. These midwinter celebrations were times of weather divination, marking the halfway point between the winter solstice and the spring equinox.

In Germany, the hedgehog served as the original animal of prognostication, symbolizing the natural world's wisdom and the promise of better days ahead. When German immigrants brought this tradition to North America, the groundhog replaced the hedgehog, becoming a local stand-in for the same symbolic role.

From its inception, the groundhog was more than a mere animal—it was a vessel for human hope. Its emergence each February became a moment of collective anticipation, a chance to dream of spring even in the depths of winter. This tradition reflects a universal human longing for certainty, comfort, and the reassurance that brighter days lie ahead.

The Groundhog and the Human Need for Hope

Hope is a powerful and universal human emotion, serving as a psychological anchor during times of difficulty or uncertainty. The groundhog's role as a symbol of hope is particularly poignant because it arrives at a critical juncture in the year, when winter often feels interminable, and the promise of spring seems distant.

1. **Seasonal Despair and the Groundhog's Reassurance:** The cold and dark of winter can weigh heavily on the human spirit, contributing to feelings of lethargy, sadness, and even seasonal affective disorder (SAD). Groundhog Day provides a moment of lightness and anticipation, offering a symbolic promise that the cycles of nature will continue and that warmth and growth are on the horizon.

2. **Hope in Ritual and Tradition:** The ritual of Groundhog Day transforms the mundane passage of time into an event imbued with meaning. By collectively watching and interpreting the groundhog's actions, communities create a shared experience of hope and optimism, reinforcing the human capacity to endure challenges and look forward to renewal.

3. **The Groundhog as a Bridge to Nature:** In an increasingly urbanized and technology-driven world, the groundhog serves as a reminder of humanity's deep connection to the natural world. Its behavior reflects the rhythms of nature, offering a sense of stability and continuity in a fast-changing world.

Cultural Representations of the Groundhog

The groundhog's emergence has inspired a wealth of cultural expressions, from folklore to modern media. Each representation emphasizes its role as a symbol of hope and renewal, highlighting its enduring resonance across generations.

1. **Folklore and Oral Traditions:** Early stories surrounding the groundhog often emphasized its wisdom and connection to the natural cycles. These tales depicted the groundhog as a mediator between the human and natural worlds, embodying the hope that humans could learn to live in harmony with the environment.

2. **Groundhog Day Celebrations:** Towns like Punxsutawney, Pennsylvania, have transformed the groundhog's role into a grand celebration. Punxsutawney Phil, the world's most famous groundhog, has become a global icon, drawing thousands of visitors and media attention each year. The joy and pageantry of these events underscore the groundhog's ability to unite people in a shared sense of optimism.

3. **Film and Popular Media:** The 1993 film *Groundhog Day* further cemented the groundhog's place in cultural consciousness. In the movie, the repetitive nature of the titular day serves as a metaphor for personal growth and the transformative power of hope. The film's themes echo the symbolic essence of the groundhog itself: the potential for renewal and the belief that change is always possible.

The Groundhog as a Symbol of Resilience

Hope and resilience are closely intertwined, and the groundhog embodies both. Its behavior—hibernating through winter and emerging at the first signs of spring—is a testament to the power of adaptation and perseverance. This biological resilience mirrors the human capacity to endure hardships and emerge stronger.

1. **Hibernation as a Metaphor:** The groundhog's ability to survive winter by conserving energy and resources offers a powerful metaphor for human resilience. It reminds us that periods of rest and introspection are not only natural but necessary for renewal and growth.

2. **Emergence as a Symbol of Triumph:** When the groundhog emerges from its burrow, it signals the end of dormancy and the beginning of action. This moment resonates deeply with those who have faced personal challenges, symbolizing the courage to step forward and embrace new opportunities.

The Groundhog in a Modern Context

In today's world, the groundhog's role as a symbol of hope takes on new significance. With climate change, global uncertainty, and societal challenges reshaping the way we live, traditions like Groundhog Day provide a comforting reminder of continuity and resilience.

1. **Environmental Awareness:** The groundhog's emergence highlights the delicate balance of ecosystems and the importance of preserving natural habitats. By honoring the groundhog as a symbol of hope, we are reminded of the need to protect the natural world that sustains us.

2. **A Beacon in Troubled Times:** The simplicity of Groundhog Day—a humble animal offering a glimpse of spring—stands in stark contrast to the complexity of modern life. Its enduring appeal lies in its ability to cut through noise and offer a moment of collective hope.

Conclusion: The Groundhog's Enduring Legacy

The groundhog's role as a symbol of hope is a testament to the human capacity to find meaning in nature and tradition. Its emergence each year offers more than a prediction of spring; it is a reminder that even in the coldest and darkest times, renewal is always possible.

As we reflect on the groundhog's significance, we see that its true power lies not in its shadow but in its ability to inspire. By looking to the groundhog, we affirm our belief in the cycles of life, the resilience of nature, and the boundless potential for renewal and growth. In the chapters that follow, we will continue to explore the rich tapestry of themes surrounding the groundhog and the enduring lessons it offers for navigating the seasons of our own lives.

Chapter 5: Preparing for the Seasons Ahead

The shifting of seasons, marked by traditions such as Groundhog Day, is a reminder of nature's cycles and the need to adapt and prepare. From the promise of spring's renewal to the challenges of winter's retreat, each season presents unique opportunities and demands. Preparation is not just about practicality—it's about aligning our actions with the rhythms of the Earth and fostering resilience and growth.

In this chapter, we explore the art of preparing for the seasons ahead, examining strategies for physical, mental, and emotional readiness. Drawing on lessons from nature, cultural practices, and modern insights, we'll uncover how to navigate seasonal transitions with intention and adaptability.

The Importance of Seasonal Preparation

Seasonal changes are more than shifts in temperature or daylight—they affect every aspect of life, from our physical surroundings to our emotional well-being. By preparing thoughtfully for these transitions, we can make the most of each season while mitigating potential challenges.

1. **Understanding Seasonal Cycles:**
   - Each season brings its own pace and priorities. Spring is a time of planting and growth, summer of abundance and activity, autumn of harvest and reflection, and winter of rest and conservation.
   - Recognizing these patterns helps us align our actions with natural rhythms, creating harmony between our environment and our lives.

2. **Building Resilience:**
   - Seasonal preparation fosters resilience by reducing the stress and uncertainty of sudden changes. From stocking supplies to setting goals, proactive planning equips us to face the future with confidence.

Practical Preparations for Seasonal Transitions

Effective preparation begins with addressing the tangible aspects of seasonal change, ensuring that our homes, communities, and routines are ready for what lies ahead.

1. **Spring: A Season of Renewal**
   - **Gardening and Agriculture:** Prepare soil for planting, choose crops suited to the season, and invest in tools for maintenance.
   - **Spring Cleaning:** Declutter living spaces to create a fresh start, symbolically clearing away the old to make room for the new.
   - **Wardrobe Transition:** Store winter clothing and bring out lighter, breathable fabrics to match rising temperatures.

2. **Summer: A Time of Activity**
   - **Energy Efficiency:** Check cooling systems and ensure homes are equipped to handle higher energy demands during hot months.
   - **Outdoor Preparedness:** Maintain gardens, prepare for outdoor activities, and stock sunscreen and insect repellents.
   - **Hydration and Health:** Emphasize hydration and light, nutritious meals to support well-being in the heat.

3. **Autumn: A Period of Harvest**
   - **Preservation and Storage:** Harvest crops, preserve food, and store resources to prepare for the scarcity of winter.
   - **Home Maintenance:** Inspect heating systems, insulate windows, and ensure roofs and gutters are ready for colder weather.
   - **Reflection and Goal Setting:** Use autumn as a time to evaluate progress and plan for the year's final quarter.

4. **Winter: A Time of Rest**
    ◦ **Emergency Supplies:** Stockpile essentials such as food, water, blankets, and flashlights in case of severe weather or power outages.
    ◦ **Energy Conservation:** Seal drafts, optimize heating, and minimize energy waste to stay warm efficiently.
    ◦ **Mental Health Support:** Combat seasonal affective disorder (SAD) with light therapy, exercise, and social connections.

Emotional and Psychological Preparation

Seasonal transitions often bring emotional and psychological shifts, influenced by changes in weather, daylight, and social activities. Preparing mentally for these transitions is as crucial as physical readiness.

1. **Mindset Shifts:**
    ◦ Embrace the strengths of each season. Spring's renewal, summer's vitality, autumn's reflection, and winter's rest all offer valuable lessons for personal growth.
    ◦ Cultivate gratitude for the unique qualities of each season, fostering a sense of appreciation rather than dread.
2. **Building Routines:**
    ◦ Establish seasonal rituals that align with personal goals and values. For example, a spring morning walk to appreciate blooming flowers or a winter evening devoted to journaling.
    ◦ Adapt daily routines to changing daylight hours and energy levels.
3. **Managing Expectations:**
    ◦ Recognize that each season may come with challenges—rainy spring days, sweltering summer heat, or winter's darkness. Accepting these realities helps reduce frustration and maintain focus on positive aspects.

Lessons from Nature: Adaptation and Growth

Nature provides a blueprint for seasonal preparation, with countless examples of adaptation and resilience in the face of change. By observing and emulating these strategies, we can enhance our ability to navigate life's transitions.

1. **Animal Behavior:**
   - **Hibernation:** Animals like bears and groundhogs conserve energy during winter, reminding us of the importance of rest and conservation in challenging times.
   - **Migration:** Birds migrate to favorable climates, teaching us the value of flexibility and seeking opportunities when circumstances change.
2. **Plant Cycles:**
   - **Seasonal Growth:** Plants adapt their growth cycles to match environmental conditions, flourishing when resources are abundant and conserving energy when they are scarce.
   - **Seed Dormancy:** Some seeds remain dormant through winter, waiting for optimal conditions to sprout, symbolizing patience and strategic timing.

Cultural Practices for Seasonal Alignment

Human traditions worldwide offer rich insights into how to prepare for and celebrate the changing seasons. Incorporating these practices into modern life can create a deeper connection to nature and community.

1. **Seasonal Festivals:**
   - Festivals like the spring equinox (Ostara), midsummer (Litha), and autumn harvests reflect humanity's reverence for seasonal cycles. Participating in or creating personal rituals can foster a sense of continuity and belonging.

2. **Cultural Wisdom:**
   - Indigenous practices often emphasize harmony with nature, such as reading environmental cues to predict seasonal changes or using sustainable methods to prepare for winter.
   - Incorporating cultural wisdom into seasonal preparation can deepen understanding and respect for the natural world.

3. **Community Connection:**
   - Seasonal traditions often involve communal activities, from harvest festivals to winter holiday gatherings. Engaging with community strengthens bonds and provides mutual support during transitions.

The Role of Reflection in Preparation

Preparation is not only forward-looking; it also involves reflecting on past seasons to learn and grow. By evaluating what worked and what didn't, we can refine our strategies and set more effective goals.

1. **Journaling and Record-Keeping:**
   - Keep a seasonal journal to document weather patterns, personal achievements, and challenges. This record can serve as a valuable resource for future planning.
2. **Celebrating Successes:**
   - Acknowledge accomplishments from the previous season, no matter how small. This practice reinforces a positive mindset and builds momentum for the future.
3. **Identifying Areas for Growth:**
   - Reflect on lessons learned and identify opportunities for improvement. For example, if winter felt particularly isolating, plan more social activities for the next year.

Conclusion: Embracing the Cycle of Seasons

Preparing for the seasons ahead is both a practical and symbolic act, reflecting our relationship with nature and our aspirations for growth. Each transition offers a chance to align with the rhythms of the Earth, adapt to new challenges, and cultivate resilience.

As we embrace the cycles of nature, we find that preparation is not just about weathering storms or welcoming sunshine—it's about living intentionally and fully in harmony with the world around us. The seasons remind us that change is inevitable, but with foresight, flexibility, and a hopeful spirit, we can face each transition with confidence and grace.

Appendix A: Seasonal Activities for Renewal

The changing seasons provide an opportunity to align our lives with the rhythms of nature. Each season brings its own energy, challenges, and opportunities for growth, making it the perfect time to engage in activities that promote renewal and balance. This appendix outlines a variety of seasonal activities designed to foster physical, mental, and emotional rejuvenation, helping individuals connect with the natural world and embrace the unique qualities of each season.

Spring: Awakening and Growth

Spring symbolizes renewal, growth, and fresh beginnings. As nature reawakens, it's a time to embrace activities that stimulate creativity, energy, and forward momentum.

1. **Gardening and Planting:**
   - Begin a garden, whether in a backyard, on a balcony, or with indoor pots.
   - Plant herbs, flowers, or vegetables that align with your personal goals (e.g., lavender for relaxation, basil for prosperity).
   - Use compost to nourish the soil, emphasizing sustainability and renewal.
2. **Spring Cleaning:**
   - Deep clean your living spaces to clear out stagnant energy and create a sense of freshness.
   - Declutter closets, donate unused items, and organize spaces to reflect the new season.
   - Incorporate natural cleaning products, such as vinegar and essential oils, for an eco-friendly touch.
3. **Outdoor Exploration:**
   - Take nature walks to observe budding flowers, birds returning from migration, and other signs of spring.
   - Visit local parks or botanical gardens to connect with the season's vibrancy.

- ◦ Practice outdoor yoga or meditation, focusing on themes of growth and renewal.

4. **Creative Pursuits:**
   - ◦ Start a journal to set intentions for the season and track progress.
   - ◦ Explore painting, crafting, or other creative hobbies that inspire growth and self-expression.
   - ◦ Write poetry or stories inspired by the themes of spring.

Summer: Vitality and Abundance

Summer is a season of energy, activity, and abundance. It's a time to celebrate life's fullness and engage in activities that maximize joy, connection, and productivity.

1. **Outdoor Activities:**
   - Host picnics or barbecues with family and friends to strengthen social connections.
   - Participate in water sports such as swimming, kayaking, or paddleboarding.
   - Plan a camping trip to immerse yourself in the season's warmth and vitality.
2. **Harvest and Foraging:**
   - Visit farmer's markets to enjoy fresh, locally grown produce.
   - Learn about foraging for edible plants in your area (with proper guidance and safety precautions).
   - Preserve fruits and vegetables through canning, freezing, or drying.
3. **Health and Wellness:**
   - Develop a fitness routine that takes advantage of the longer daylight hours, such as morning runs or evening bike rides.
   - Focus on hydration and nourishing meals featuring fresh, seasonal ingredients.
   - Practice mindfulness by journaling outdoors, observing sunsets, or listening to nature sounds.
4. **Community Engagement:**
   - Attend summer festivals, fairs, or concerts to celebrate the season with others.

- Volunteer for local environmental cleanups or community gardens.
- Organize a block party or neighborhood event to foster connection and collaboration.

Autumn: Reflection and Harvest

Autumn is a time of transition, inviting reflection, gratitude, and preparation for the colder months. It's a season to embrace activities that balance productivity with introspection.

1. **Seasonal Crafts:**
   - Create autumn-themed decorations, such as wreaths made of dried leaves, pinecones, or acorns.
   - Carve pumpkins or make jack-o'-lanterns to celebrate harvest traditions.
   - Experiment with preserving leaves or pressing flowers for creative projects.

2. **Culinary Exploration:**
   - Bake seasonal treats like apple pies, pumpkin bread, or spiced cookies.
   - Learn to cook hearty soups and stews using fall vegetables such as squash and root crops.
   - Host a potluck featuring autumn-inspired dishes.

3. **Reflection and Goal-Setting:**
   - Write in a gratitude journal to focus on the abundance in your life.
   - Reflect on accomplishments from the year and set intentions for the remainder of the year.
   - Participate in mindfulness exercises, such as meditating on the beauty of falling leaves or writing about personal growth.

4. **Seasonal Decor and Rituals:**
   - Decorate your home with warm, autumnal colors and natural elements like gourds or dried corn.
   - Celebrate harvest festivals or cultural traditions that honor the season's bounty.

- Create a seasonal altar with symbols of gratitude and abundance, such as candles, fruits, and photographs.

Winter: Rest and Restoration

Winter is a time for rest, introspection, and deep renewal. It encourages activities that conserve energy, nurture the spirit, and prepare for the coming spring.

1. **Comfort and Coziness:**
   - Embrace hygge, the Danish concept of creating a cozy atmosphere, with soft blankets, warm lighting, and comforting drinks like hot cocoa or herbal tea.
   - Spend evenings by the fireplace reading or knitting.
   - Invest in indoor plants to bring life into your home during the colder months.

2. **Personal Development:**
   - Explore self-improvement through online courses, workshops, or books.
   - Practice journaling, focusing on themes of rest, introspection, and setting goals for the new year.
   - Experiment with new hobbies or revisit old ones, such as drawing, sewing, or playing an instrument.

3. **Mindful Rest:**
   - Prioritize sleep and establish a calming bedtime routine.
   - Practice restorative yoga or meditation to cultivate peace and relaxation.
   - Engage in reflective practices such as writing down lessons learned during the year.

4. **Seasonal Festivities:**
   - Celebrate winter holidays with family and friends, incorporating traditions that bring joy and warmth.
   - Host a game night or movie marathon featuring cozy, feel-good themes.

○ Attend or organize a solstice celebration to honor the turning of the seasons.

Activities That Transcend Seasons

Some activities are beneficial year-round, helping you stay connected to the cycles of nature and maintain a balanced lifestyle.

1. **Nature Journaling:**
   ○ Record observations about the changing environment, including weather patterns, plant growth, and animal behavior.
   ○ Reflect on how seasonal changes affect your mood, energy, and daily routines.
2. **Seasonal Mindfulness Practices:**
   ○ Perform meditations focused on seasonal themes (e.g., planting intentions in spring, embracing abundance in summer).
   ○ Use breathing exercises to center yourself during seasonal transitions.
3. **Community Connection:**
   ○ Join local groups or organizations focused on gardening, environmental preservation, or cultural celebrations.
   ○ Share seasonal traditions and activities with others to strengthen bonds and create lasting memories.

Conclusion

Seasonal activities for renewal allow us to align with the natural world, foster personal growth, and embrace the unique opportunities each season offers. By engaging in these practices, we can nurture our well-being, deepen our connection to nature, and find joy in the rhythm of life's ever-changing cycles. Let this appendix serve as a guide to living intentionally through the seasons, making the most of each phase in your journey of renewal.

<u>Message from the Author:</u>

I hope you enjoyed this book, I love astrology and knew there was not a book such as this out on the shelf. I love metaphysical items as well. Please check out my other books:

-Life of Government Benefits

-My life of Hell

-My life with Hydrocephalus

-Red Sky

-World Domination:Woman's rule

-World Domination:Woman's Rule 2: The War

-Life and Banishment of Apophis: book 1

-The Kidney Friendly Diet

-The Ultimate Hemp Cookbook

-Creating a Dispensary(legally)

-Cleanliness throughout life: the importance of showering from childhood to adulthood.

-Strong Roots: The Risks of Overcoddling children

-Hemp Horoscopes: Cosmic Insights and Earthly Healing

- Celestial Hemp Navigating the Zodiac: Through the Green Cosmos

-Astrological Hemp: Aligning The Stars with Earth's Ancient Herb

-The Astrological Guide to Hemp: Stars, Signs, and Sacred Leaves

-Green Growth: Innovative Marketing Strategies for your Hemp Products and Dispensary

-Cosmic Cannabis

-Astrological Munchies

-Henry The Hemp

-Zodiacal Roots: The Astrological Soul Of Hemp

- **Green Constellations: Intersection of Hemp and Zodiac**

-Hemp in The Houses: An astrological Adventure Through The Cannabis Galaxy

-Galactic Ganja Guide

Heavenly Hemp
Zodiac Leaves
Doctor Who Astrology
Cannastrology
Stellar Satvias and Cosmic Indicas
<u>Celestial Cannabis: A Zodiac Journey</u>
AstroHerbology: The Sky and The Soil: Volume 1
AstroHerbology:Celestial Cannabis:Volume 2
Cosmic Cannabis Cultivation
The Starry Guide to Herbal Harmony: Volume 1
The Starry Guide to Herbal Harmony: Cannabis Universe: Volume 2

Yugioh Astrology: Astrological Guide to Deck, Duels and more
Nightmare Mansion: Echoes of The Abyss
Nightmare Mansion 2: Legacy of Shadows
Nightmare Mansion 3: Shadows of the Forgotten
Nightmare Mansion 4: Echoes of the Damned
The Life and Banishment of Apophis: Book 2
Nightmare Mansion: Halls of Despair
<u>Healing with Herb: Cannabis and Hydrocephalus</u>
<u>Planetary Pot: Aligning with Astrological Herbs: Volume 1</u>
Fast Track to Freedom: 30 Days to Financial Independence Using AI, Assets, and Agile Hustles
<u>Cosmic Hemp Pathways</u>
How to Become Financially Free in 30 Days: 10,000 Paths to Prosperity
Zodiacal Herbage: Astrological Insights: Volume 1
Nightmare Mansion: Whispers in the Walls
The Daleks Invade Atlantis
Henry the hemp and Hydrocephalus

10X The Kidney Friendly Diet
Cannabis Universe: Adult coloring book

The Boogey Book

Locked In Reflection: A Chastity Journey Through Locktober

Generating Wealth Quickly:

How to Generate $100,000 in 24 Hours

Star Magic: Harness the Power of the Universe

The Flatulence Chronicles: A Fart Journal for Self-Discovery

The Doctor and The Death Moth

Seize the Day: A Personal Seizure Tracking Journal

The Ultimate Boogeyman Safari: A Journey into the Boogie World and Beyond

Whispers of Samhain: 1,000 Spells of Love, Luck, and Lunar Magic: Samhain Spell Book

Apophis's guides:

Witch's Spellbook Crafting Guide for Halloween

<u>Frost & Flame: The Enchanted Yule Grimoire of 1000 Winter Spells</u>

<u>The Ultimate Boogey Goo Guide & Spooky Activities for Halloween Fun</u>

Harmony of the Scales: A Libra's Spellcraft for Balance and Beauty

The Enchanted Advent: 36 Days of Christmas Wonders

Nightmare Mansion: The Labyrinth of Screams

Harvest of Enchantment: 1,000 Spells of Gratitude, Love, and Fortune for Thanksgiving

The Boogey Chronicles: A Journal of Nightly Encounters and Shadowy Secrets

The 12 Days of Financial Freedom: A Step-by-Step Christmas Countdown to Transform Your Finances

Sigil of the Eternal Spiral Blank Journal

A Christmas Feast: Timeless Recipes for Every Meal

Holiday Stress-Free Solutions: A Survival Guide to Thriving During the Festive Season

Whispers of the Harvest: The Corn Mother's Journal

The Evergreen Spellbook

The Doctor Meets the Boogeyman

The White Witch of Rose Hall's SpellBook

The Gingerbread Golem's Shadow: A Study in Sweet Darkness

The Gingerbread Golem Codex: An Academic Exploration of Sweet Myths

The Gingerbread Golem Grimoire: Sweet Magicks and Spells for the Festive Witch

The Curse of the Gingerbread Golem

10-minute Christmas Crafts for kids

<u>Christmas Crisis Solutions: The Ultimate Last-Minute Survival Guide</u>

Gingerbread Golem Recipes: Holiday Treats with a Magical Twist

The Infinite Key: Unlocking Mystical Secrets of the Ages

Enchanted Yule: A Wiccan and Pagan Guide to a Magical and Memorable Season

Dinosaurs of Power: Unlocking Ancient Magick

Astro-Dinos: The Cosmic Guide to Prehistoric Wisdom

Gallifrey's Yule Logs: A Festive Doctor Who Cookbook

The Dino Grimoire: Secrets of Prehistoric Magick

The Gift They Never Knew They Needed

The Gingerbread Golem's Culinary Alchemy: Enchanting Recipes for a Sweetly Dark Feast

A Time Lord Christmas: Holiday Adventures with the Doctor

Krampusproofing Your Home: Defensive Strategies for Yule

Silent Frights: A Collection of Christmas Creepypastas to Chill Your Bones

Santa Raptor's Jolly Carnage: A Dino-Claus Christmas Tale

Prehistoric Palettes: A Dino Wicca Coloring Journey

The Christmas Wishkeeper Chronicles

The Starlight Sleigh: A Holiday Journey

Elf Secrets: The True Magic of the North Pole

Reclaiming Time: How to Live More by Doing Less

Chronovore: The Eternal Nexus

The Mind Reset: Unlocking Your Inner Peace in a Chaotic World

Confidence Code: Building Unshakable Self-Belief

Baby the Vampire Terrier

Baby the Vampire Terrier's Christmas Adventure

Celestial Streams: The Content Creator's Astrology Manual

The Wealth Whisperer: Unlocking Abundance with Everyday Actions

The Energy Equation: Maximize Your Output Without Burning Out

The Happiness Algorithm: Science-Backed Steps to Joyful Living

Stress-Free Success: Achieving Goals Without Anxiety

Mindful Wealth: The New Blueprint for Financial Freedom

The Festive Flavors of New Year: A Culinary Celebration

The Master's Gambit: Keys of Eternal Power

Shadowed Secrets: Groundhog Day Mysteries

Beneath the Burrow: Lessons from the Groundhog

If you want solar for your home go here: https://www.harborso-lar.live/apophisenterprises/

Get Some Tarot cards: https://www.makeplayingcards.com/sell/
apophis-occult-shop

Get some shirts: https://www.bonfire.com/store/apophis-shirt-emporium/

<u>**Instagrams:**</u>
@apophis_enterprises,
@apophisbookemporium,
@apophisscardshop
Twitter: @apophisenterpr1
Tiktok:@apophisenterprise
Youtube: @sg1fan23477, @FiresideRetreatKingdom
Hive: @sg1fan23477
CheeLee: @SG1fan23477

Podcast: Apophis Chat Zone: https://open.spotify.com/show/
5zXbrCLEV2xzCp8ybrfHsk?si=fb4d4fdbdce44dec

Newsletter: https://apophiss-newsletter-27c897.beehiiv.com/

If you want to support me or see posts of other projects that I have come over to: **buymeacoffee.com/mpetchinskg**

I post there daily several times a day

Get your Dinowicca or Christmas themed digital products, especially Santa Raptor songs and other musics. Here: **https://sg1fan23477.gumroad.com**

Apophis Yuletide Digital has not only digital Christmas items, but it will have all things with Dinowicca as well as other Digital products.

www.ingramcontent.com/pod-product-compliance
Lightning Source LLC
Chambersburg PA
CBHW072050150726
47996CB00015B/2469